DOG DAYS

PREVIOUS BOOKS BY JULIE LUMSDEN

Naked by Profession, Leafe Press, 2000
Sixteen Poems, Open House Editions, 2004
True Crime, Shoestring Press, 2011

DOG DAYS

JULIE LUMSDEN

All rights reserved. No part of this work covered by the copyright herein may be reproduced or used in any means – graphic, electronic, or mechanical, including copying, recording, taping, or information storage and retrieval systems – without written permission of the publisher.

Printed by imprintdigital
Upton Pyne, Exeter
www.digital.imprint.co.uk

Typesetting and cover design by The Book Typesetters
us@thebooktypesetters.com
07422 598 168
www.thebooktypesetters.com

Published by Shoestring Press
19 Devonshire Avenue, Beeston, Nottingham, NG9 1BS
(0115) 925 1827
www.shoestringpress.co.uk

First published 2022
© Copyright: Julie Lumsden
© Cover art: Vivian Jackson
© Author photograph: MRJ

The moral right of the author has been asserted.

ISBN 978-1-915553-04-1

To Michael

ACKNOWLEDGEMENTS

Acknowledgements are due to the following journals where some of these poems first appeared: *The Frogmore Papers*, *Matter*, *Mslexia*, *The North*, *Pennine Platform*, *Poetry News*, *The Rialto*, *Stand*, *Smiths Knoll*, *Tears in the Fence*, and *Litter* (www).

Also the following anthologies: *Millstone Grit: Poets associated with Sheffield Hallam University* (2016); *One for the Road: an anthology of pubs and poetry* (smith|doorstep, 2017); *The Result is What You See Today: Poems about Running* (smith|doorstep, 2019); *The Ver Prize 2020*; *Strike Up the Band: Poems for John Lucas at 80*.

And some of these poems, or versions of them, first appeared in pamphlets published by Leafe Press and Shoestring.

CONTENTS

Sermon	1
Wildlife Documentary	2
Wonderful Tennessee	3
Godot	4
Day Trip	5
Cherish	6
The Forever House	7
Territorial Haunting	8
The Big Question	9
Inner Space	10
Nine Lives	11
Haiku for the Duration	12
Haiku for England	13
Endgame	14
Dash	15
Horoscope	16
Keep the Show on the Road	17
Summer in the University Library	18
The Cheap Hotel	19
Once upon a Time	20
Domestic Science Lesson, 1959	21
Fancy Man	22
Real Drama	23
The Fortune Teller	23
The Best Friend	24
The Witness	25
The Policeman	26
The Hangman	27
The Doorman	28

Fortune Teller	29
Escape to the Country	30
Covert Crescent	31
Not Loving Thy Neighbour	32
Christina the Astonishing Arrives in Covert Crescent to Prepare the Faithful for the End of Days	33
Pub Talk	34
Theology	35
We All Have Our Way	36
Satan's Gift	37
Until the Fat Lady Sings	38
The Wall	39
Haworth	40
Postcard to Haworth	41
Café Talk	42
Love from Another Country	43
Mother	44
The Slow Death of a Poet	45
Death of an Actor	46
An Actor's Life for Me	47
Leading Part	48
Equal Billing	49
Death of a Dramatist	50
Precious Little	51
What My New Neighbour Told Me	52
Dog Days	53

SERMON

Only the Guilty Species needs forgiveness.
Pray for the world's working animals.
Avoid films where cowboy horses fall over.
Pity the mother of the world, milked to death, calling
for the disappeared.
Be anthropomorphic when noticing beetle scurrying to safety.
Read the Bible, where unclean spirits
are transferred from a lunatic
into terrified swine which dash into a lake.
Understand that the trashing of a perfectly designed pangolin
is violence against God.
Beware of evil outliving nature, give up plastic for Lent.
Be a quick fish for information.
Know that the devil is always in the details
(discuss with Sunni & Shia, Catholic, etcetera).
Grow out of detail. Find serenity –
lazy dog enjoying the end of the world.

WILDLIFE DOCUMENTARY

Nothing is interesting in my life except other people.
– George Sand, letter to Flaubert

Distant relatives
display affection, annoyance, empathy
in their apish way.
Also regard the ingenuity of frogs, their enemies (my tribe)
creating habitat destruction
which means they may lose their home (pond)
necessary for breeding.
Courtship begins with an elegant arm wave.
Midges, nettle flowers, the stillness of this Derbyshire
pond under a clump of alder trees.
Yes, yes, look, look –
a creature on two legs, primeval bouncer, frog
walking on water.

WONDERFUL TENNESSEE
Distillation of a play by Brian Friel, first performed at The Abbey Theatre, Dublin, on 30 June 1993.

Silence. Sound —
waves tumbling over each other, seagull,
singing, laughing, as three couples run onto the beach.
They are celebrating the birthday of Terry.
Angela and Berna are sisters. Angela and George are having
a secret affair. Frank hopes to stay off the booze.
Trish never stops dancing. Half way

into the Second Act — Terry declares
his medical condition and expectation of demise.
Six monologues. Then they make a promise.
A year from now they will return for another celebration,
all of them, Terry will be with them, Terry will always
be with them. Laughing, singing, they leave
human litter on the beach. Silence.

GODOT

A play about nothing
and everything. Ah, the gloriously simple
truth of it –

no point in discussing
Waiting, unless you wish to philosophise.
I'm just remembering

dear Hubert – fine actor, whose recent
resting
proved briefer than he envisaged.

DAY TRIP

In a pub full of all day drinkers, a joke
I couldn't catch
set the table laughing –

one of those days
I couldn't drift or flow

or forget the serious sea
out in the bay where the tide comes in
faster than a man can run.

CHERISH

a beach
      where two stones
pummel and smooth
one another
to sand, rolled by a tide
they cannot alter.

THE FOREVER HOUSE

For so many years we've been practising old age.
A preoccupation with coats and the suitability of carrier bags.
I seem to have lost the knack
of inhabiting that small space between the future and the past.
I know I've become morbid, continually
searching for him, watching him
in every room. He's such a quiet man, unlike that loud father
silenced. The dead know nothing or everything, mute
on the subject of where years go and why.

TERRITORIAL HAUNTING

The living-room door
suddenly closing, firmly, purposefully

with real intention
and we'd been arguing of course

and stopped. I sensed
a kindly authority, surveillance, approval

of our attachment
to this place. There it is again –

unexplained laughter.

THE BIG QUESTION

The trick of the afterlife –
what you sign up for, you get?

The home of the righteous
in gardens of delight?

Leisure enough for awareness
of the thing we made of it?

I am sorry for that mistake
in 1989 but what is there in my life

for which I am not sorry?
We are not saints

but we keep our appointment
here, on time, released

from waiting. And Godot says
'don't let me keep you'?

INNER SPACE

Is it true that after returning
from the moon – one astronaut
discovered God, the second
found alcohol and the third
had a nervous breakdown?

I concentrate on the near and small.
An ant on a stone. A cobweb.
My strange self. We all have
interesting organs working hard
in a place we hope never to see.

NINE LIVES

You and I talk the sun down. It is enough
this. Fifty years
under five roofs, we are home to
ourselves. Sometimes we hate each other
for less than a moment.

Open the back door
for eyes bigger than the round moon, cat
never needs calling back. And you and I
step outside to stand on our pocket of grass
with nowhere to slink to.

HAIKU FOR THE DURATION

Duvet afternoon –
rescue cat curled perfectly
unfazed by lockdown.

HAIKU FOR ENGLAND

Fish and chip supper.
Third Sunday after Easter.
Soft midsummer rain.

ENDGAME

The cave is crowded.
Three women in prayer shawls.

Flies are dying like people.
Someone has seen the sun.

Trees plummet downward.
The weather is king.

King of kings, which
sacrilege doomed us?

The universe
catching itself around

one particular foray?
Wetlands return, water

has its victory.
The ocean heaves

like the serpent of chaos.
We have given up

hug times. Five-a-day
is a thing of the past.

We need the sun to bake
our dead. Bad hair days.

A gun speaks in the street
to empty houses.

DASH

That summer of drought, months
of sad city dust. Then, suddenly

buckets of rain

and Crazy Cal steps out of his shoes,
strips himself of jeans, tee shirt

and runs fast

right to the top of Mansfield Road
for the joy of it.

HOROSCOPE

Littered under Mercury –
I deal in doubles and neither partner
is short changed
for who is to say we love less
by loving more.

KEEP THE SHOW ON THE ROAD

Our Two Hander suits us.
So what makes us change the script? Do we require
Exposition? Complication? Crisis?

We bring in another character.

Its comforting to learn that a particular species of penguin
displays an elaborate bowing ritual to reinforce
a lifelong bond, also

keenly adulterous and brutal to rivals.

SUMMER IN THE UNIVERSITY LIBRARY

Jack looks up from
Seven Theories of Human Nature

to watch the girl opposite, scanning the shelf —
a deep stain under the arm of her yellow T-shirt.

Philosophy
is a study of people with their clothes on.

THE CHEAP HOTEL

Climbing into bed
after so long, Frank's hand flickers
over his arm, as if he could conceal
'Kate' in a heart.
We were in Tenerife he says
and we were drunk.
Does her arm say 'Frank'?
No, she went for the Celtic Knot.
I'm discreet

about a body
fit now only for myself. Body and I
are old friends, cheerfully
accommodating
each other's complaints.
I'm looking after her. I especially enjoy
dressing her.

Dear Body,
stay well, stay
through this final fiasco
to meet up
in our wardrobe mirror
where I will lift a breast in my palm,
determine its weight, acknowledge
the heart beneath it, envelop
your winters and wounds
in clean colours.

Despite your
increasing demand for attention
and the interest of consultants,
your fakery and pretence.
I love you
you ramshackle slut, my one
and only.

ONCE UPON A TIME

Kitty and I run laughing all the way along Woolwich High Road
to take our Junior Bronze Ballroom in the arms
of our lounge-lizard instructors
knowing it wouldn't matter if our feet never touched the floor.
Mum had made me a blue dress, a lacy affair
with pleats set in from the shoulders.
Kitty's was green with a V-neck.
Inept as we were, we both passed with honours,
a quick-step followed by a tango leaving us flushed and giddy.

DOMESTIC SCIENCE LESSON, 1959

How To Wash Up. Collect the dirty dishes and remove
    any food.
Arrange neatly in piles on one side of the sink or bowl.
    Half fill
the bowl with very hot water, and, using a soap shaker,
    make the
water soapy. Wash one dish at a time, beginning with
    the cleanest
articles. Have a second bowl of hot water, and rinse each
    dish after
washing. Invert on the draining board, and wipe dry with
    a clean
tea towel. The hotter the water and the drier the tea towel
    the less
likely are the dishes to have a smeared appearance. Burns
    or stains
should be rubbed with dry salt. Wash and scald the dish
    cloth, and
hang in the open air. *I never believed work was worship until this.*

FANCY MAN

A matinee that Saturday – watching Dirk,
bad and beautiful in *The Blue Lamp*. Beauty
is never comfortable, and in a man
of course, entirely gratuitous.
What can you do with it? Gaze at it,
guard it, fuck it, outstare it, wait
for it to fade or thicken into something easier to bear.

REAL DRAMA

The Fortune Teller
   – postwar depression in Brixton –

Friday afternoons at the Oxo factory,
the women have had enough

make do and mend. They want something
for themselves: *Lets have a look dear…..*

this youngster, skinny, short-sighted, plain
as hell, trying not to laugh

her little neck
bent forward over the cards.

Looking down, I read the future clear,
her skull is fragile as a tea cup.

The Best Friend
— Gosh dear, now you've done it —

Photographer's model
at the Camera Club,

done up to the nines
as hostess,

acting, always acting
with clients

and getting an agent —
Background Artiste

we got sent up for films.
Lady Godiva Rides Again

stills photograph shows
Ruth, 4th on the left

in a line-up of beauty queens
alongside Diana Dors

and Joan Collins, a starlet
who made it.

Four years later, Ruth
makes a name for herself.

The Witness
– The Magdala public house –

Face down on the pavement, blood mixing with
the flagon of beer he'd been carrying – a slow foam

frothing like wash day. Someone shouted
Look what you've done Ruth. She was

waiting against the wall
for whatever would happen next, her pale head

floating in the light from the pub window.
Composed, was the word my friend used

when we all flowed out to see what the fuss was about.
What an Easter that was –

Mum with the cancer, Kenny in Cyprus,
another landlord forcing us into a midnight flit.

She looked refined, smart, a nice grey two-piece.
Someone took the gun from her hand. I think

she may have been empty then, a spent thing, patient
with a strange kind of happiness.

The Policeman
   – off duty –

I did notice a face
wreathed by the sign *wines & spirits* –

not unusual for a woman to
look through the saloon bar window

to see if her bloke is there.
After the commotion, I went outside

to approach a woman
looking down at the body of a man.

Phone the police, she said. *I am a police officer*
I said, removing the gun from her right hand.

While we waited for the police car
I offered her a cigarette. *No thank you,* she said.

The Hangman
– *sunshine, the Test Match, jazz* –

I hanged them both.
The one before Mrs Ellis, I hanged her also.

I made this point to the army of reporters
waiting to interview me

after the event. No one remembers
or was interested

in Mrs Christofi, hanged eight months earlier
for butchering her daughter in law.

No one wept or chanted through the night for
Mrs Christofi, or broke through a police cordon

to bang on the great wooden double doors,
begging her to pray with them.

Of course there wasn't much passion in that one,
a lot of brutality, but not what you might call

an *interesting* passion. Let's put it this way,
she wasn't the sort of woman

men apologise to with roses.
She was older, not much of a looker.

The Doorman
– high class members only –

Did you ever have an obsession
you were glad to reach the end of?

Mine was Johnny Metcalf, a dead
unreliable bastard. What is it

about a particular hand holding a cigarette?
In any room he only had to look my way

for it to start up again,
like booze, like drugs, a trap

neither of us could escape. Except
I'm past it now and Johnny

never gets up from Brighton.
I used to do pencil sketches of the staff

and clientele. They all had to sign the book,
socialites, politicians, gangsters, the motor racing boys –

David Blakely, dark eyes
to die for, but always under the influence

and causing aggravation at the bar.
And businessman, Desmond Cusson –

solid, the type you can rely on – did you know
he took care of her son's school fees?

Ruth Ellis, Manageress, The Little Club, 1953
– sketch captures her heyday you might say.

FORTUNE TELLER

If you know what people want, you know
everything about them. This one
is afraid that the best is over.

What can I say?

The next seven years will be no better
and no worse than the last.
Adopt an ugly cat for luck.

ESCAPE TO THE COUNTRY
*On 10 August 3003 the temperature in London
exceeded a hundred degrees for the first time*

That apocalyptic summer, buildings going up, trees coming down.
Day after day, nowhere to hide.
A police helicopter banks and circles, lower and lower
every sleepless night. The heat is on until November
and doesn't end with a firework called The End of the World.

That's when we decide to move to the edge, and yes,
dusk happens here
and trees which disappear into the night. There is much to
      appreciate
in a line of white birds flying east, crossing
a shadow moving west. The rustic gate. The low crime rate.
My wellingtons are waiting in the hall.
Just now, standing motionless as a hare, at an upstairs window
in the good dark, I suddenly think of Madame Bovary –
She wanted to die, and she wanted to live in Paris.
Dear God, please save me from long walks of appreciation.

COVERT CRESCENT

At this remove, she's uncertain whether she played Ophelia
at the National or in her head.

There is no reason not to live here
except for the racing clouds reflected in the windows.

At dusk, on the patio, barefoot in a floating nightdress
she gestures in the spot of her security light.

NOT LOVING THY NEIGHBOUR

Hacking through a wild paradise to replace hawthorn
with concrete,
removing the silver birch.

Clocking my dressing gown
at midday
over the low fence which makes bad neighbours.

CHRISTINA THE ASTONISHING ARRIVES IN COVERT CRESCENT TO PREPARE THE FAITHFUL FOR THE END OF DAYS

Oh Lord, where am I? Who is this man following me
from room to room? Yesterday he led me to the Health Centre –
the five wounds of my stigmata sparking fire.
The Friday Passion sent me cawing to the rafters. Father Anthony
emails the Vatican about my knowledge of twelfth century Latin –
he cocks his head to one side, that way he has, eyes bluer than
Mary's robe. I have tried not to let my eyes return to him
even in the bits he sits out. The Mass is not what it was. During
what they call their Sign of Peace, a woman attempting to hug me
was blown the length of the church by my reluctant sigh.
How may I prepare these people for the shattering? I'm not
        so much
sickened by the stench of sin as shocked by the paltriness
of their concerns. How may I live the ordinary stuff of days,
        who have
flown higher than the sucking mouths of angels, through
a crack in the universe to plunge my fist into a pulsating heart?

PUB TALK

Let's have a drink says Bob
so we bowl into the Crafty Fox

where Daisy tells us she's become a Buddhist
and Jo says that she once saw

the Dalai Lama interviewed, surprised
when he seemed to suggest

that the *practicality* of faith is best found
in one's own culture

and Bob says that Indian mysticism didn't free
George Harrison from Benson&Hedges.

Tom doesn't say much (still in a quandary regarding
partner who never wants to hear from him again)

and Kieran tells me, so quietly, that his grandfather
is now laid out with a rosary laced among his fingers.

Having no wish to hear any criticism of belief –
I defend Jo when she happily combines evolution

with God separating land from sea in seven days.
Bob asks Daisy if she's going to contemplate her navel.

THEOLOGY

When the young priest with dark eyes
suggested that Heaven was simply
God's *space* —

she felt she needed a little more to go on —
the smell of lilies perhaps, a waxed floor,
white doves bearing billet-doux
from a pale bridegroom.

WE ALL HAVE OUR WAY

Sally has sixty three handbags.
Chris sets off for another writing retreat.
Dave indulges his booze habit.
My television flickers into life –

Eva Braun's Home Movies,
back to back comedy, the collapse
of some far away country.

SATAN'S GIFT

Sensibility. Alertness
without pressure, nerves,
regrets, fear, boredom
or desire. You are everything
to yourself. Peace of mind
for the taking – heroin
giving us back to ourselves
as babies, before we knew
we needed to be born.

UNTIL THE FAT LADY SINGS

They arrange to meet, late afternoon,
hidden corner of an empty bar
so Jack rolls up in defiance of the law.
He doesn't disagree that the world is
divided into smokers and non-smokers
and they get into a feisty conversation
about Georgie Best and Jesus
and genetics and virtue
and the concept of the addictive personality.
Jill loves the chance to scold him again
and watch his slim fingers sifting the Amber Leaf.
Suddenly she punches him
and he takes it, the way a man must.
They stare at beer mats. He puts his hand
on her hand. She doesn't move.

THE WALL

'Oppressive' was a word
Ted Hughes used about this valley
although he loved it. On the right road,
I take a footpath to Heptonstall –
ten times longer like a kind of Yorkshire joke –
narrower, steeper, leading
to a towering slice of granite,
black, slicked with rain, a haunt
with its low local graffiti.
For some time now, I've been smacked
up against a wall

looking our for signs
and landmarks and a wider view.
Wearing the green waterproof
of our holiday together, I miss
Jack, with him I'd have walked
differently because he kept me graceful.
When I reach Heptonstall, the rain stops.
Of course we'd have loved
the Sylvia Plath thing, the grave
with its offerings of beads and totems
and then we'd have chosen
The Cross Inn and The White Lion.

HAWORTH

This is where we sat
and wrote, and to the right –
that was the sofa
one of us died on.

These thimble books,
impossible to read, grew
into Heathcliff
who has no pity

he tells us.
Emily knew herself
as a girl
and iron man, never

made a friend, unable
to meet the eyes of
neighbours, unsociable
even at home.

My sister, the watcher,
watched by a watcher
she calls Whacher
or Thou –

sometimes, at night
close to Thou
she experiences
'a sweetness that proved us one'.

Enough words.
Let's rouse the dogs, hit the moor
as fame, postcard fame
travels toward us –

POSTCARD TO HAWORTH

Why is Jane Eyre's rival
    Blanche Ingram
"reprehensibly foolish"
for desiring a well-dressed
      social life?

CAFÉ TALK

Your favourite poems
packed fat
while I prefer brevity –
as few words as possible,
particular, precise, neat
on a wide white page.
We give the cheese rolls
full marks for nutritional
value, none for presentation.
You smooth a piece of hair
into that fine line
along your brow.

I love your blue shirt –
lapiz-lazuli

I *flirt* with the word.

LOVE FROM ANOTHER COUNTRY

Dearest, our Christmas catch-up
bringing your dislike of the traditional.
Well, I approve of a new bank holiday
for the Queen's Platinum Jubilee.
What are we without God, king and country customs
on what's left of the green and pleasant?
I want rites of passage in ancient places, fine words
linking the newly born, nearly departed, gone –
a farewell made beautiful with ceremony.
(Thank you for the nuisance of having to devise
a funeral procedure for a card-carrying atheist.)
      You loved our forsaken churches
rooted. Spotting the spire of All Saints
showed us we were almost home.
        Things have changed since you left.
Next door are extending again.
The Old Queen's Head has become a heritage centre.
Travellers Rest is Tesco.
      Isuko sent me a snow-kissed robin.

MOTHER
I tell you, hopeless grief is passionless
— Elizabeth Barret Browning, sonnets

Gave her life to us,
would have died for us —
no tenderness, praise, and a history
like her, living
on no words. Did tell me
once, suddenly —
that she was engaged at nineteen
and they came into her workplace
to tell her he'd been killed
while riding his motorcycle.
Twelve years later, she married
and got me. How strange

to live a parallel life. Life
pulled back
from where it was going
in that pause
between the Somme
and Normandy: *we'll meet again*
unsung. Now, I think of her
in my garden — eyes closed, face
to the sun, smiling.
She died alone.
Regarding attachment theory —
ask my child.

THE SLOW DEATH OF A POET

The poetry scene is showbiz without first night parties:
names, photographs, biographies – the writing community
talking to itself and making a song and dance of it.
Agents who provide venues – Literature Development Officers
encouraging performance by poets who are bad
at reading aloud in public. Poetry World is showbusiness

slower. I send five poems to a leading journal for consideration –
three years later – acceptance, named on front cover – stardom.
Quit while you're ahead. Curtains. The problem is
encouragement. How can one abandon the struggle
for preferment? Never the favourite child:
You're Not Watching Me, Mummy

DEATH OF AN ACTOR

Out of drama school, first job, Equity –
unfortunately I'm unable to use my real name
because someone else has it. I am

Jelly Lumsden

for a while. Until a tragically sad event
suddenly leaves my name free.

AN ACTOR'S LIFE FOR ME

So much analysis, discussion about this character and his world. Did Hamlet sleep with Ophelia? Only on the tour, darling.

LEADING PART

I played Her Indoors
with George Cole in Minder.

Also Mrs Mainwaring
(but not in the film).

EQUAL BILLING

In a recent production of Krapps Last Tape –
my name is placed

prominently

in the programme –
Derek Jacoby's cardigan was knitted by me.

DEATH OF A DRAMATIST

Mike says all you've got is a boring couple,
old people at that, talking, nothing happening,
you need forty five story events. Forty five?
Okay Mike, how about one of them gets up
and opens the window. What does that tell us?
It's a hot night. What are you showing us?
Restlessness, stress, tension, after all they've got
a heroin addict son who has a prostitute girlfriend.
Now we're getting somewhere, heroin, girl, addict,
sex worker, that's good, give us the girl, the girl
is a gift, what does she do? But Mike, it's not her story,
its about the parents. That's boring, a married couple
lying in bed talking, that's not drama, give me
events. Look…get her round with the son,
they break in, smash the place up, steal money,
beat up the old couple, and then…the Dad
recognises the girl because he's picked her up
in the red light district…I can't do that Mike, you see
I just want the parents to lie there, wondering
what went wrong with their lives. I want to listen
to what they have to say while they watch the dawn
slowly reach them, filling the room with light.
The lighting would be superb Mike.

PRECIOUS LITTLE

Superseded twin, ghost
of an earlier self, suspects
I've gone a bit simple, seeing as I know
that in this given, extra time
since I came back to the living –
God gifted me
a semi-rural cottage with a walk-to hospital
close to a church spire encircled by cafés, trees
continually surprising me

with blessedness.
Today we stroll to our co-op in autumn sunshine
and come back to find Wendy Cope
on the mat.
Waiting for tea to brew, I'm simply
observing our tiny front garden
twigs framing a singular rose in November.
– *Ah, for how long?*
Yes, this question which poets have done to death.
Keep it simple. Keep it between
forever and ever, and me.

WHAT MY NEW NEIGHBOUR TOLD ME

That God is silent.
That she's been a widow for seventeen years.
That growing old is to want less, and to like it.
That she misses her husband.
That cleanliness is next to godliness but beware of bleach.
That television is a window.
That Tony Blair is a trickster. That her social life
is being a fly on the Coronation Street wall.
That no one gets away with anything.
That old age is a load of pills.
That mice, rats, hedgehogs, badgers, elephants and
earthworms are the meek who will inherit the world.
That, next time, she is going to be party girl.
That silence is answer enough.

DOG DAYS

Dogwood and I are happy now
  nothing in our midsummer garden wants to be more
or less, neither trying hard nor giving up.
  Lying flat on grass, I
am shorter than dogwood, as low as dandelion, above us –
  God's leafy choreography.
A nameless insect negotiates my hand.
  All flesh is grass. Dogwood agrees.